SENECA

ON A HAPPY LIFE

Published by Brolga Publishing Pty Ltd
ABN 46 063 962 443

PO Box 452
Torquay Victoria 3228
Australia

email: markzocchi@brolgapublishing.com.au

National Library of Australia
Cataloguing-in-Publication data
        Seneca, author.
        ISBN 9781920785949 (paperback)

A catalogue record for this book is available from the National Library of Australia

Printed in Australia
Cover design by Brolga Publishing
Typesetting by Elly Cridland
        aeledapublishingservices

BE PUBLISHED

Publish through a successful publisher
National Distribution to Australia & New Zealand
International Distribution to the United Kingdom
Ebooks Worldwide
Sales Representation to South East Asia

Email: markzocchi@brolgapublishing.com.au

SENECA

ON A HAPPY LIFE

CONTENTS

FOREWORD

For most of my reading life, I have been inspired to connect with philosophies and ancient teachings about life and how to live well.

In 2018, I was listening to a podcast by an author speaking about Stoicism.

Stoicism? I had heard the word 'stoic', meaning someone who was strong and uncomplaining but I was unfamiliar with the philosophy of Stoicism.

I began investigating further and reading the works of Marcus Aurelius, Zeno, Cicero, Epictetus and Seneca.

These authors were mostly quite reluctant to have their works read, usually writing for themselves, but I found their words to be inspiring, offering ways to live a good life that are as relevant today as when they were originally written.

Practises such as focusing on what you can

control in your life and therefore, the things you can do something about, rather than worrying about all the things that are out of your control. This is often the root of our suffering: being entangled in our **thoughts** about the world rather than living in the world **as it is**.

Shakespeare said: Nothing is good or bad, it is thinking that makes it so.

And so it is that the stoics constantly remind themselves of the reality of life, that we are born and we will die.

Seneca especially talks about not wasting our life and considering that every moment that passes is the death of a part of our life, never to be had again. This is not being morbid, rather it becomes a motivation to live, whatever life we have, well.

Stoicism is just as beneficial in this world of pandemics and uncertainty as it was in Seneca's lifetime in Imperial Rome.

Modern day stoics include Admiral James Stockdale, who was a POW for over seven years during the Vietnam War; Nelson Mandela, political activist, revolutionary and first president of South Africa; and modern day adventurer, Ross Edgley, the first person to swim around Great Britain. Edgley wrote about his world record experience and his unique brand of 'stoic sports science'.

My motivation and hope in presenting this edition of Seneca's writing on what makes a happy life is that you too will be inspired to live a happy life for your benefit and that of others.

Mark Zocchi
Brolga Publishing
2021

ABOUT THE AUTHOR

Lucius Annaeus Seneca, or Seneca the Younger, as he is also known, is regarded as one of the most influential Stoics in history, second only to Roman Emperor Marcus Aurelius. He was born in Hispania, southern Spain, around 4 BC and raised and educated in Rome. He was schooled in rhetoric and philosophy and had a career in politics and law.

In 41 AD he was exiled to the island of Corsica, accused of adultery with the emperor's niece. He was freed after 8 years to return to Rome to tutor the future emperor, Nero. In a bizarre twist of fate, it was Nero who later, convinced that Seneca was plotting against him, ordered his former tutor to commit suicide. Seneca met his death according to the philosophy with which he had lived his life, with a calmness of mind and body.

CHAPTER I

OF A HAPPY LIFE,
AND WHEREIN IT CONSISTS

"... enjoy the present without any anxious dependence upon the future. Not to amuse ourselves with either hopes or fears, but to rest satisfied with what we have, which is abundantly sufficient; for he that is so, wants nothing."

There is not any thing in this world, perhaps, that is more talked of, and less understood, than the business of a happy life. It is every man's wish and design; and yet not one of a thousand that knows wherein that happiness consists. We live, however, in a blind and eager pursuit of it; and the more haste we make in a wrong way, the further we are from our journey's end. Let us therefore, first, consider "what it is we should be at;" and, secondly, "which is the readiest way to compass it." If we be right, we shall find every day how much we improve; but if we either follow the cry, or the track, of people that are out of the way, we must expect to be misled, and to continue our days in wandering in error. Wherefore, it highly concerns us to take along with us a skilful guide; for it is not in this, as in other voyages, where the highway brings us to our place of repose; or if a man should happen to be out, where the inhabitants might set him right again: but on the contrary, the beaten road is here the most dangerous, and the people, instead of helping us, misguide us. Let us not therefore follow, like beasts, but rather govern ourselves by reason, than by example. It fares with us in human life as in a routed army; one stumbles first, and then another falls upon him, and so they follow, one upon the neck of another, until the whole field comes to be but one heap of miscarriages.

And the mischief is, "that the number of the multitude carries it against truth and justice;" so that we must leave the crowd, if we would be happy: for the question of a happy life is not to be decided by vote: nay, so far from it, that plurality of voices is still an argument of the wrong; the common people find it easier to believe than to judge, and content themselves with what is usual, never examining whether it be good or not. By the common people is intended the man of title as well as the clouted shoe: for I do not distinguish them by the eye, but by the mind, which is the proper judge of the man. Worldly happiness, I know, makes the head giddy; but if ever a man comes to himself again, he will confess, "Whatsoever he has done, he wishes undone;" and that "the things he feared were better than those he prayed for."

The true happiness of life is to be free from perturbations, to understand our duties towards God and man: to enjoy the present without any anxious dependence upon the future. Not to amuse ourselves with either hopes or fears, but to rest satisfied with what we have, which is abundantly sufficient; for he that is so, wants nothing. The great blessings of mankind are within us, and within our reach; but we shut our eyes, and, like people in the dark, we fall foul upon the very thing, which we search for without finding it. "Tranquillity is a certain equality of mind, which no condition of fortune can either exalt or depress." Nothing can make it less: for it is the state of human perfection: it raises us as high as we can go; and makes every man his own supporter; whereas he that is borne up by any thing else may fall. He that judges aright, and perseveres in it, enjoys a perpetual calm: he takes a true prospect of things; he observes an order, measure, a decorum in all his actions; he has a benevolence in his nature; he squares his life according to reason; and draws to himself love and admiration. Without a certain and an unchangeable judgment, all the rest is but fluctuation: but "he that always wills and nills the same thing, is undoubtedly in the right." Liberty and serenity of mind must necessarily ensue upon the mastering of those things, which either allure or affright us; when instead of those flashy pleasures, (which even at the best are both vain and hurtful together,) shall find ourselves possessed of joy transporting and everlasting. It must be a sound mind that makes a happy man; there must be constancy in all conditions, a care for the things of this world, but without trouble; and such an indifferency for the bounties of fortune, that either with them, or without them, we may live contentedly.

There must be neither lamentation, nor quarrelling, nor sloth, nor fear; for it makes a discord in a man's life. "He that fears, serves." The joy of a wise man stands firm without interruption; in all places, at all times, and in all conditions, his thoughts are cheerful and quiet. As it never came in to him from without, so it will never leave him; but it is born within him, and inseparable from him. It is a solicitous life that is egged on with the hope of any thing, though never so open and easy, nay, though a man should never suffer any sort of disappointment. I do not speak this either as a bar to the fair enjoyment of lawful pleasures, or to the gentle flatteries of reasonable expectations: but, on the contrary, I would have men to be always in good humour, provided that it arises from their own souls, and be cherished in their own breasts. Other delights are trivial; they may smooth the brow, but they do not fill and affect the heart.

"True joy is a serene and sober motion;" and they are miserably out that take laughing for rejoicing. The seat of it is within, and there is no cheerfulness like the resolution of a brave mind, that has fortune under his feet. He that can look death in the face, and bid it welcome; open his door to poverty, and bridle his appetites; this is the man whom Providence has established in the possession of inviolable delights. The pleasures of the vulgar are ungrounded, thin, and superficial; but the others are solid and eternal. As the body itself is rather a necessary thing, than a great; so the comforts of it are but temporary and vain; beside that, without extraordinary moderation, their end is only pain and repentance; whereas a peaceful conscience, honest thoughts, virtuous actions, and an indifference for casual events, are blessings without end, satiety, or measure. This consummated state of happiness is only a submission to the dictate of right nature; "The foundation of it is wisdom and virtue; the knowledge of what we ought to do, and the conformity of the will to that knowledge."

CHAPTER II

HUMAN HAPPINESS IS FOUNDED UPON WISDOM AND VIRTUE; AND FIRST, OF WISDOM

"A wise man ... is not moved with the utmost violence of fortune, nor with the extremities of fire and sword; whereas a fool is afraid of his own shadow, and surprised at ill accidents, as if they were all levelled at him."

Taking for granted that human happiness is founded upon wisdom and virtue we shall treat of these two points in order as they lie: and, first, of wisdom; not in the latitude of its various operations but as it has only a regard to good life, and the happiness of mankind.

Wisdom is a right understanding, a faculty of discerning good from evil; what is to be chosen, and what rejected; a judgment grounded upon the value of things, and not the common opinion of them; an equality of force, and a strength of resolution. It sets a watch over our words and deeds;

it takes us up with the contemplation of the works of nature, and makes us invincible by either good or evil fortune. It is large and spacious, and requires a great deal of room to work in; it ransacks heaven and earth; it has for its object things past and to come, transitory and eternal. It examines all the circumstances of time; "what it is, when it began, and how long it will continue: and so for the mind; whence it came; what it is; when it begins; how long it lasts; whether or not it passes from one form to another, or serves only one and wanders when it leaves us; whether it abides in a state of separation, and what the action of it; what use it makes of its liberty; whether or not it retains the memory of things past, and comes to the knowledge of itself." It is the habit of a perfect mind, and the perfection of humanity, raised as high as Nature can carry it. It differs from philosophy, as avarice and money; the one desires, and the other is desired; the one is the effect and the reward of the other. To be wise is the use of wisdom, as seeing is the use of eyes, and well-speaking the use of eloquence. He that is perfectly wise is perfectly happy; nay, the very beginning of wisdom makes life easy to us.

Neither is it enough to know this, unless we print it in our minds by daily meditation, and so bring a good-will to a good habit. And we must practice what we preach: for philosophy is not a subject for popular ostentation; nor does it rest in words, but in things. It is not an entertainment taken up for delight, or to give a taste to our leisure; but it fashions the mind, governs our actions, tells us what we are to do, and what not. It sits at the helm, and guides us through all hazards; nay, we cannot be safe without it, for every hour gives us occasion to make use of it. It informs us in all duties of life, piety to our parents, faith to our friends, charity to the miserable, judgment in counsel; it gives us peace by fearing nothing, and riches by coveting nothing.

There is no condition of life that excludes a wise man from discharging his duty. If his fortune be good, he tempers it; if bad, he masters it; if he has an estate, he will exercise his virtue in plenty; if none, in poverty: if he cannot do it in his country, he will do it in banishment; if he has no command, he will do the office of a common soldier. Some people have the skill of reclaiming the fiercest of beasts; they will make a lion embrace his keeper, a tiger kiss him, and an elephant kneel to him. This is the case of a wise man in the extremest difficulties; let them be never so terrible in themselves, when they come to him once, they are perfectly tame. They that ascribe the invention of tillage, architecture, navigation, etc., to wise men, may perchance be in the right, that they were invented by wise men, as wise men; for wisdom does not teach our fingers, but our minds: fiddling and dancing, arms and fortifications, were the works of luxury and discord; but wisdom instructs us in the way of nature, and in the arts of unity and concord, not in the instruments, but in the government of life; not to make us live only, but to live happily.

She teaches us what things are good, what evil, and what only appear so; and to distinguish betwixt true greatness and tumour. She clears our minds of dross and vanity; she raises up our thoughts to heaven, and carries them down to hell: she discourses of the nature of the soul, the powers and faculties of it; the first principles of things; the order of Providence: she exalts us from things corporeal to things incorporeal, and retrieves the truth of all: she searches nature, gives laws to life; and tells us, "That it is not enough to God, unless we obey him:" she looks upon all accidents as acts of Providence: sets a true value upon things; delivers us from false opinions, and condemns all pleasures that are attended with repentance. She allows nothing to be good that will not be so forever; no man to be happy but that needs no other happiness than what he has within himself. This is the happiness of human life; a happiness that can neither be corrupted nor extinguished: it inquires into the nature of the heavens, the influence of the stars; how far they operate upon our minds and bodies: which thoughts, though they do not form our manners, they do yet raise and dispose us for glorious things.

It is agreed upon all hands that "right reason is the perfection of human nature," and wisdom only the dictate of it. The greatness that arises from it is solid and unmovable, the resolutions of wisdom being free, absolute and constant; whereas folly is never long pleased with the same thing, but still shifting of counsels and sick of itself.

There can be no happiness without constancy and prudence, for a wise man is to write without a blot, and what he likes once he approves for ever. He admits of nothing that is either evil or slippery, but marches without staggering or stumbling, and is never surprised; he lives always true and steady to himself, and whatsoever befalls him, this great artificer of both fortunes turns to advantage; he that demurs and hesitates is not yet composed; but wheresoever virtue interposes upon the main, there must be concord and consent in the parts; for all virtues are in agreement, as well as all vices are at variance. A wise man, in what condition so ever he is will be still happy, for he subjects all things to himself, because he submits himself to reason, and governs his actions by council, not by passion.

He is not moved with the utmost violence of fortune, nor with the extremities of fire and sword; whereas a fool is afraid of his own shadow, and surprised at ill accidents, as if they were all levelled at him. He does nothing unwillingly, for whatever he finds necessary, he makes it his choice. He propounds to himself the certain scope and end of human life: he follows that which conduces to it, and avoids that which hinders it. He is content with his lot whatever it be, without wishing what he has not, though, of the two, he had rather abound than want. The great business of his life like that of nature is performed without tumult or noise. He neither fears danger or provokes it, but it is his caution, not any want of courage — for captivity, wounds and chains, he only looks upon as false and lymphatic terrors. He does not pretend to go through with whatever he undertakes, but to do that well which he does. Arts are but the servants — wisdom commands — and where the matter fails it is none of the workman's fault. He is cautelous in doubtful cases, in prosperity temperate, and resolute in adversity, still making the best of every condition and improving all occasions to make them serviceable to his fate. Some accidents there are, which I confess may affect him, but not overthrow him, as bodily pains, loss of children and friends, the ruin and desolation of a man's country. One must be made of stone or iron, not to be sensible of these calamities; and, beside, it were no virtue to bear them, if a body did not feel them.

There are three degrees of proficients in the school of wisdom. The first are those that come within sight of it, but not up to it — they have learned what they ought to do, but they have not put their knowledge in practice — they are past the hazard of a relapse, but they have still the grudges of a disease, though they are out of the danger of it. By a disease I do understand an obstinacy in evil, or an ill habit, that makes us over eager upon things which are either not much to be desired, or not at all. A second sort are those that have subjected their appetites for a season, but are yet in fear of falling back. A third sort are those that are clear of many vices but not of all. They are not covetous, but perhaps they are choleric

— nor lustful, but perchance ambitious; they are firm enough in some cases but weak enough in others: there are many that despise death and yet shrink at pain. There are diversities in wise men, but no inequalities — one is more affable, another more ready, a third a better speaker; but the happiness of them all is equal. It is in this as in heavenly bodies, there is a certain state in greatness.

In civil and domestic affairs, a wise man may stand in need of counsel, as of a physician, an advocate, a solicitor; but in greater matters, the blessing of wise men rests in the joy they take in the communication of their virtues. If there were nothing else in it, a man would apply himself to wisdom, because it settles him in a perfect tranquillity of mind.

CHAPTER III.

THERE CAN BE NO HAPPINESS
WITHOUT VIRTUE.

"Nothing can be good which gives neither greatness nor security to the mind; but, on the contrary, infects it with insolence, arrogance, and tumour: nor does virtue dwell upon the tip of the tongue, but in the temple of a purified heart."

Virtue is that perfect good which is the complement of a happy life; the only immortal thing that belongs to mortality — it is the knowledge both of others and itself — it is an invincible greatness of mind, not to be elevated or dejected with good or ill fortune. It is sociable and gentle, free, steady, and fearless, content within itself, full of inexhaustible delights, and it is valued for itself. One may be a good physician, a good governor, a good grammarian, without being a good man, so that all things from without are only accessories, for the seat of it is a pure and holy mind. It consists in a congruity of actions which we can never expect so long as we are distracted by our passions: not but that a man may be allowed to change colour and countenance, and suffer such impressions as are properly a kind of natural force upon the body, and not under the dominion of the mind; but all this while I will have his judgment firm, and he shall act steadily and boldly, without wavering betwixt the motions of his body and those of his mind.

It is not a thing indifferent, I know, whether a man lies at ease upon a bed, or in torment upon a wheel — and yet the former may be the worse of the two if he suffer the latter with honour, and enjoy the other with infamy. It is not the matter, but the virtue, that makes the action good or ill; and he that is led in triumph may be yet greater than his conqueror.

When we come once to value our flesh above our honesty we are lost: and yet I would not press upon dangers, no, not so much as upon inconveniences, unless where the man and the brute come in competition; and in such a case, rather than make a forfeiture of my credit, my reason, or my faith, I would run all extremities.

They are great blessings to have tender parents, dutiful children, and to live under a just and well-ordered government. Now, would it not trouble even a virtuous man to see his children butchered before his eyes, his father made a slave, and his country overrun by a barbarous enemy? There is a great difference betwixt the simple loss of a blessing and the succeeding of a great mischief in the place of it over and above. The loss of health is followed with sickness, and the loss of sight with blindness; but this does not hold in the loss of friends and children, where there is rather something to the contrary to supply that loss: that is to say, virtue, which fills the mind, and takes away the desire of what we have not. What matters it whether the water be stopped or not, so long as the fountain is safe? Is a man ever the wiser for a multitude of friends, or the more foolish for the loss of them? so neither is he the happier, nor the more miserable.

Short life, grief and pain are accessions that have no effect at all upon virtue. It consists in the action and not in the things we do — in the choice itself, and not in the subject-matter of it. It is not a despicable body or condition, nor poverty, infamy or scandal, that can obscure the glories of virtue; but a man may see her through all oppositions: and he that looks diligently into the state of a wicked man will see the canker at his heart, through all the false and dazzling splendours of greatness and fortune. We shall then discover our childishness, in setting our hearts upon things trivial and contemptible, and in the selling of our very country and parents for a rattle. And what is the difference (in effect) betwixt old men and children, but that the one deals in paintings and statues, and the other in babies, so that we ourselves are only the more expensive fools.

If one could but see the mind of a good man, as it is illustrated with virtue; the beauty and the majesty of it, which is a dignity not so much as to be thought of without love and veneration — would not a man bless himself at the sight of such an object as at the encounter of some supernatural power — a power so miraculous that it is a kind of charm upon the souls of those that are truly affected with it. There is so wonderful a grace and authority in it that even the worst of men approve it, and set up for the reputation of being accounted virtuous themselves. They covet the fruit indeed, and the profit of wickedness; but they hate and are ashamed of the imputation of it. It is by an impression of Nature that all men have a reverence for virtue — they know it and they have a respect for it though they do not practice it — nay, for the countenance of their very wickedness, they miscall it virtue. Their injuries they call benefits, and expect a man should thank them for doing him a mischief — they cover their most notorious iniquities with a pretext of justice.

He that robs upon the highway had rather find his booty than force it; ask any of them that live upon rapine, fraud, oppression, if they had not rather enjoy a fortune honestly gotten, and their consciences will not suffer them to deny it. Men are vicious only for the proof of villainy; for at the same time that they commit it they condemn it; nay, so powerful is virtue, and so gracious is Providence, that every man has a light set up within him for a guide, which we do, all of us, both see and acknowledge, though we do not pursue it. This it is that makes the prisoner upon the torture happier than the executioner, and sickness better than health, if we bear it without yielding or repining — this it is that overcomes ill-fortune and moderates good — for it marches betwixt the one and the other, with an equal contempt for both. It turns (like fire) all things into itself, our actions and our friendships are tinctured with it, and whatever it touches becomes amiable.

That which is frail and mortal rises and falls, grows, wastes, and varies from itself; but the state of things divine is always the same; and so is virtue, let the matter be what it will. It is never the worse for the difficulty of the action, nor the better for the easiness of it. It is the same in a rich man as in a poor; in a sickly man as in a sound; in a strong as in a weak; the virtue of the besieged is as great as that of the besiegers. There are some virtues, I confess, which a good man cannot be without, and yet he had rather have no occasion to employ them. If there were any difference, I should prefer the virtues of patience before those of pleasure; for it is braver to break through difficulties than to temper our delights. But though the subject of virtue may possibly be against nature, as to be burnt or wounded, yet the virtue itself of an invincible patience is according to nature. We may seem, perhaps, to promise more than human nature is able to perform; but we speak with a respect to the mind, and not to the body.

If a man does not live up to his own rules, it is something yet to have virtuous meditations and good purposes, even without acting; it is generous, the very adventure of being good, and the bare proposal of an eminent course of life, though beyond the force of human frailty to accomplish. There is something of honour yet in the miscarriage; nay, in the naked contemplation of it. I would receive my own death with as little trouble as I would hear of another man's; I would bear the same mind whether I be rich or poor, whether I get or lose in the world; what I have, I will neither sordidly spare, or prodigally squander away, and I will reckon upon benefits well-placed as the fairest part of my possession: not valuing them by number or weight, but by the profit and esteem of the receiver; accounting myself never the poorer for that which I give to a worthy person. What I do shall be done for conscience, not ostentation.

I will eat and drink, not to gratify my palate, or only to fill and empty, but to satisfy nature: I will be cheerful to my friends, mild and placable to my enemies: I will prevent an honest request if I can foresee it, and I will grant it without asking: I will look upon the whole world as my country, and upon the gods, both as the witnesses and the judges of my words and deeds. I will live and die with this testimony, that I loved good studies, and a good conscience; that I never invaded another man's liberty; and that I preserved my own. I will govern my life and my thoughts as if the whole world were to see the one, and to read the other; for "what does it signify to make anything a secret to my neighbour, when to God (who is the searcher of our hearts) all our privacies are open?"

Virtue is divided into two parts, contemplation and action. The one is delivered by institution, the other by admonition: one part of virtue consists in discipline, the other in exercise: for we must first learn, and then practice. The sooner we begin to apply ourselves to it, and the more haste we make, the longer shall we enjoy the comforts of a rectified mind; nay, we have the fruition of it in the very act of forming it: but it is another sort of delight, I must confess, that arises from a contemplation of a soul which is advanced into the possession of wisdom and virtue. If it was so great a comfort to us to pass from the subjection of our childhood into a state of liberty and business, how much greater will it be when we come to cast off the boyish levity of our minds, and range ourselves among the philosophers?

We are past our minority, it is true, but not our

indiscretions; and, which is yet worse, we have the authority of seniors, and the weaknesses of children, (I might have said of infants, for every little thing frights the one, and every trivial fancy the other.) Whoever studies this point well will find that many things are the less to be feared the more terrible they appear. To think anything good that is not honest, were to reproach Providence; for good men suffer many inconveniences; but virtue, like the sun, goes on still with her work, let the air be never so cloudy, and finishes her course, extinguishing likewise all other splendours and oppositions; insomuch that calamity is no more to a virtuous mind, than a shower into the sea. That which is right, is not to be valued by quantity, number, or time; a life of a day may be as honest as a life of a hundred years: but yet virtue in one man may have a larger field to show itself in than in another.

One man, perhaps, may be in a station to administer unto cities and kingdoms; to contrive good laws, create friendships, and do beneficial offices to mankind.

For virtue is open to all; as well to servants and exiles, as to princes: it is profitable to the world and to itself, at all distances and in all conditions; and there is no difficulty can excuse a man from the exercise of it; and it is only to be found in a wise man, though there may be some faint resemblances of it in the common people. The Stoics hold all virtues to be equal; but yet there is great variety in the matter they have to work upon, according as it is larger or narrower, illustrious or less noble, of more or less extent; as all good men are equal, that is to say, as they are good; but yet one may be young, another old; one may be rich, another poor; one eminent and powerful, another unknown and obscure.

There are many things, which have little or no grace in themselves, and are yet glorious and remarkable by virtue. Nothing can be good which gives neither greatness nor security to the mind; but, on the contrary, infects it with insolence, arrogance, and tumour: nor does virtue dwell upon the tip of the tongue, but in the temple of a purified heart. He that depends upon any other good becomes covetous of life, and what belongs to it; which exposes a man to appetites that are vast, unlimited, and intolerable. Virtue is free and indefatigable, and accompanied with concord and gracefulness; whereas pleasure is mean, servile, transitory, tiresome, and sickly and scarce outlives the tasting of it: it is the good of the belly, and not of the man; and only the happiness of brutes. Who does not know that fools enjoy their pleasures, and that there is great variety in the entertainments of wickedness? Nay, the mind itself has its variety of perverse pleasures as well as the body: as insolence, self-conceit, pride, garrulity, laziness, and the abusive wit of turning everything into ridicule, whereas virtue weighs all this, and corrects it. It is the knowledge both of others and of itself; it is to be learned from itself; and the very will itself may be taught; which will cannot be right, unless the whole habit of the mind be right from whence the will comes. It is by the impulse of virtue that we love virtue, so that the very way to virtue, lies by virtue, which takes in also, at a view, the laws of human life.

Neither are we to value ourselves upon a day, or an hour, or any one action, but upon the whole habit of the mind. Some men do one thing bravely, but not another; they will shrink at infamy, and bear up against poverty: in this case, we commend the fact, and despise the man. The soul is never in the right place until it be delivered from the cares of human affairs; we must labour and climb the hill, if we will arrive at virtue, whose seat is upon the top of it. He that masters avarice, and is truly good, stands firm against ambition; he looks upon his last hour not as a punishment, but as the equity of a common fate; he that subdues his carnal lusts shall easily keep himself untainted with any other: so that reason does not encounter this or that vice by itself, but beats down all at a blow. What does he care for ignominy that only values himself upon conscience, and not opinion?

Socrates looked a scandalous death in the face with the same constancy that he had before practiced towards the thirty tyrants: his virtue consecrated the very dungeon: as Cato's repulse was Cato's honour, and the reproach of the government. He that is wise will take delight even in an ill opinion that is well gotten; it is ostentation, not virtue, when a man will have his good deeds published; and it is not enough to be just where there is honour to be gotten, but to continue so, in defiance of infamy and danger.

But virtue cannot lie hid, for the time will come that shall raise it again (even after it is buried) and deliver it from the malignity of the age that oppressed it: immortal glory is the shadow of it, and keeps it company whether we will or not; but sometimes the shadow goes before the substance, and other whiles it follows it; and the later it comes, the larger it is, when even envy itself shall have given way to it. It was a long time that Democritus was taken for a madman, and before Socrates had any esteem in the world. How long was it before Cato could be understood? Nay, he was affronted, contemned, and rejected; and the people never knew the value of him until they had lost him: the integrity and courage of mad Rutilius had been forgotten but for his sufferings. I speak of those that fortune has made famous for their persecutions: and there are others also that the world never took notice of until they were dead; as Epicurus and Metrodorus, that were almost wholly unknown, even in the place where they lived.

Now, as the body is to be kept in upon the downhill, and forced upwards, so there are some virtues that require the rein and others the spur. In liberality, temperance, gentleness of nature, we are to check ourselves for fear of falling; but in patience, resolutions, and perseverance, where we are to mount the hill, we stand in need of encouragement. Upon this division of the matter, I had rather steer the smoother course than pass through the experiments of sweat and blood: I know it is my duty to be content in all conditions; but yet, if it were at my election, I would choose the fairest. When a man comes once to stand in need of fortune, his life is anxious, suspicious, timorous, dependent upon every moment, and in fear of all accidents.

How can that man resign himself to God, or bear his lot, whatever it be, without murmuring, and cheerfully submit to Providence that shrinks at every motion of pleasure or pain? It is virtue alone that raises us above griefs, hopes, fears and chances; and makes us not only patient, but willing, as knowing that whatever we suffer is according to the decree of Heaven. He that is overcome with pleasure, (so contemptible and weak an enemy) what will become of him when he comes to grapple with dangers, necessities, torments, death, and the dissolution of nature itself? Wealth, honour, and favour, may come upon a man by chance; nay, they may be cast upon him without so much as looking after them: but virtue is the work of industry and labour; and certainly it is worth the while to purchase that good which brings all others along with it. A good man is happy within himself, and independent upon fortune: kind to his friend, temperate to his enemy, religiously just, indefatigably laborious; and he discharges all duties with a constancy and congruity of actions.

CHAPTER IV

PHILOSOPHY IS
THE GUIDE OF LIFE

"... let me understand that the good
of life does not consist in the length
or space; but in the use of it."

If it be true, that the understanding and the will
are the two eminent faculties of the reasonable
soul, it follows necessarily, that wisdom and virtue,
(which are the best improvements of these two
faculties,) must be the perfection also of our
reasonable being; and consequently, the undeniable
foundation of a happy life. There is not any duty
to which Providence has not annexed a blessing;
nor any institution of Heaven which, even in
this life, we may not be the better for; not any
temptation, either of fortune or of appetite, that
is not subject to our reason; nor any passion or
affliction for which virtue has not provided a
remedy. So that it is our own fault if we either fear
or hope for anything; which two affections are the

root of all our miseries. From this general prospect of the foundation of our tranquillity, we shall pass by degrees to a particular consideration of the means by which it may be procured, and of the impediments that obstruct it; beginning with that philosophy which principally regards our manners, and instructs us in the measures of a virtuous and quiet life.

Philosophy is divided into moral, natural, and rational: the first concerns our manners; the second searches the works of Nature; and the third furnishes us with propriety of words and arguments, and the faculty of distinguishing, that we may not be imposed upon with tricks and fallacies. The causes of things fall under natural philosophy, arguments under rational, and actions under moral. Moral philosophy is again divided into matter of justice, which arises from the estimation of things and of men; and into affections and actions; and a failing in any one of these, disorders all the rest: for what does it profit us to know the true value of things, if we be transported by our passion? or to master our appetites without understanding the when, the what, the how, and other circumstances of our proceedings? For it is one thing to know the rate and dignity of things, and another to know the little nicks and springs of acting. Natural philosophy is conversant about things corporeal and incorporeal; the disquisition of causes and effects, and the contemplation of the cause of causes. Rational philosophy is divided into logic and rhetoric; the one looks after words, sense, and order; the other treats barely of words, and the significations of them. Socrates places all philosophy in morals; and wisdom in the distinguishing of good and evil.

It is the art and law of life, and it teaches us what to do in all cases, and, like good marksmen, to hit the white at any distance. The force of it is incredible; for it gives us in the weakness of a man the security of a spirit: in sickness it is as good as a remedy to us; for whatsoever eases the mind is profitable also to the body. The physician may prescribe diet and exercise, and accommodate his rule and medicine to the disease, but it is philosophy that must bring us to a contempt of death, which is the remedy of all diseases. In poverty it gives us riches, or such a state of mind as makes them superfluous to us. It arms us against all difficulties: one man is pressed with death, another with poverty; some with envy, others are offended at Providence, and unsatisfied with the condition of mankind: but philosophy prompts us to relieve the prisoner, the infirm, the necessitous, the condemned; to show the ignorant their errors, and rectify their affections.

It makes us inspect and govern our manners; it rouses us where we are faint and drowsy: it binds up what is loose, and humbles in us that which is contumacious: it delivers the mind from the bondage of the body, and raises it up to the contemplation of its divine original. Honours, monuments, and all the works of vanity and ambition are demolished and destroyed by time; but the reputation of wisdom is venerable to posterity, and those that were envied or neglected in their lives are adored in their memories, and exempted from the very laws of created nature, which has set bounds to all other things. The very shadow of glory carries a man of honour upon all dangers, to the contempt of fire and sword; and it were a shame if right reason should not inspire as generous resolutions into a man of virtue.

Neither is philosophy only profitable to the public, but one wise man helps another, even in the exercise of the virtues; and the one has need of the other, both for conversation and counsel; for they kindle a mutual emulation in good offices. We are not so perfect yet, but that many new things remain still to be found out, which will give us the reciprocal advantages of instructing one another: for as one wicked man is contagious to another, and the more vices are mingled, the worse it is, so is it on the contrary with good men and their virtues. As men of letters are the most useful and excellent of friends, so are they the best of subjects; as being better judges of the blessings they enjoy under a well-ordered government, and of what they owe to the magistrate for their freedom and protection. They are men of sobriety and learning, and free from boasting and insolence; they reprove the vice without reproaching the person; for they have learned to be without either pomp or envy. That which we see in high mountains, we find in philosophers; they seem taller near at hand than at a distance. They are raised above other men, but their greatness is substantial. Nor do they stand upon tiptoe that they may seem higher than they are, but, content with their own stature, they reckon themselves tall enough when fortune cannot reach them. Their laws are short, and yet comprehensive too, for they bind all.

It is the bounty of nature that we live; but of philosophy that we live well, which is in truth a greater benefit than life itself. Not but that philosophy is also the gift of Heaven, so far as to the faculty, but not to the science; for that must be the business of industry. No man is born wise; but wisdom and virtue require a tutor, though we can easily learn to be vicious without a master. It is philosophy that gives us a veneration for God, a charity for our neighbour, that teaches us our duty to Heaven, and exhorts us to an agreement one with another; it unmasks things that are terrible to us, assuages our lusts, refutes our errors, restrains our luxury, reproves our avarice, and works strangely upon tender natures.

I could never hear Attalus upon the vices of the age and the errors of life, without a compassion for mankind; and in his discourses upon poverty, there was something methought that was more than human.

"More than we use," says he, "is more than we need, and only a burden to the bearer." That saying of his put me out of countenance at the superfluities of my own fortune. And so in his invectives against vain pleasures, he did at such a rate advance the felicities of a sober table, a pure mind, and a chaste body that a man could not hear him without a love for continence and moderation. Upon these lectures of his, I denied myself, for a while after, certain delicacies that I had formerly used: but in a short time I fell to them again, though so sparingly, that the proportion came little short of a total abstinence.

Now, to show you how much earnester my entrance upon philosophy was than my progress, my tutor Sotion gave me a wonderful kindness for Pythagoras, and after him for Sextius: the former forbore shedding of blood upon his metempsychosis: and put men in fear of it, lest they should offer violence to the souls of some of their departed friends or relations. "Whether," says he, "there be a transmigration or not; if it be true, there is no hurt; if false, there is frugality: and nothing is gotten by cruelty neither, but the cozening a wolf, perhaps, or a vulture, of a supper."

Now, Sextius abstained upon another account, which was, that he would not have men inured to hardness of heart by the laceration and tormenting of living creatures; beside, "that Nature had sufficiently provided for the sustenance of mankind without blood." This wrought upon me so far that I gave over eating of flesh, and in one year I made it not only easy to me but pleasant; my mind me thought was more at liberty, (and I am still of the same opinion,) but I gave it over nevertheless; and the reason was this: it was imputed as a superstition to the Jews, the forbearance of some sorts of flesh, and my father brought me back again to my old custom, that I might not be thought tainted with their superstition. Nay, and I had much ado to prevail upon myself to suffer it too. I make use of this instance to show the aptness of youth to take good impressions, if there be a friend at hand to press them. Philosophers are the tutors of mankind; if they have found out remedies for the mind, it must be our part to employ them.

I cannot think of Cato, Lelius, Socrates, Plato, without veneration: their very names are sacred to me. Philosophy is the health of the mind; let us look to that health first, and in the second place to that of the body, which may be had upon easier terms; for a strong arm, a robust constitution, or the skill of procuring this, is not a philosopher's business. He does some things as a wise man, and other things as he is a man; and he may have strength of body as well as of mind; but if he runs, or casts the sledge, it were injurious to ascribe that to his wisdom which is common to the greatest of fools. He studies rather to fill his mind than his coffers; and he knows that gold and silver were mingled with dirt, until avarice or ambition parted them. His life is ordinate, fearless, equal, secure; he stands firm in all extremities, and bears the lot of his humanity with a divine temper.

There is a great difference betwixt the splendour of philosophy and of fortune; the one shines with an original light, the other with a borrowed one; beside that it makes us happy and immortal: for learning shall outlive palaces and monuments.

The house of a wise man is safe, though narrow; there is neither noise nor furniture in it, no porter at the door, nor anything that is either vendible or mercenary, nor any business of fortune, for she has nothing to do where she has nothing to look after. This is the way to Heaven which Nature has chalked out, and it is both secure and pleasant; there needs no train of servants, no pomp or equipage, to make good our passage; no money or letters of credit, for expenses upon the voyage; but the graces of an honest mind will serve us upon the way, and make us happy at our journey's end.

To tell you my opinion now of the liberal sciences; I have no great esteem for any thing that terminates in profit or money; and yet I shall allow them to be so far beneficial, as they only prepare the understanding without detaining it. They are but the rudiments of wisdom, and only then to be learned when the mind is capable of nothing better, and the knowledge of them is better worth the keeping than the acquiring. They do not so much as pretend to the making of us virtuous, but only to give us an aptitude of disposition to be so. The grammarian's business lies in a syntax of speech; or if he proceed to history, or the measuring of a verse, he is at the end of his line; but what signifies a congruity of periods, the computing of syllables, or the modifying of numbers, to the taming of our passions, or the repressing of our lusts? The philosopher proves the body of the sun to be large, but for the true dimensions of it we must ask the mathematician: geometry and music, if they do not teach us to master our hopes and fears, all the rest is to little purpose.

What does it concern us which was the elder of the two, Homer or Hesiod? or which was the taller, Helen or Hecuba? We take a great deal of pains to trace Ulysses in his wanderings, but were it not time as well spent to look to ourselves that we may not wander at all? Are not we ourselves tossed with tempestuous passions? And both assaulted by terrible monsters on the one hand, and tempted by syrens on the other?

Teach me my duty to my country, to my father, to my wife, to mankind. What is it to me whether Penelope was honest or not? Teach me to know how to be so myself, and to live according to that knowledge. What am I the better for putting so many parts together in music, and raising a harmony out of so many different tones? Teach me to tune my affections, and to hold constant to myself. Geometry teaches me the art of measuring acres; teach me to measure my appetites, and to know when I have enough; teach me to divide with my brother, and to rejoice in the prosperity of my neighbour. You teach me how I may hold my own, and keep my estate; but I would rather learn how I may lose it all, and yet be contented. "It is hard," you will say, "for a man to be forced from the fortune of his family." This estate, it is true, was my father's; but whose was it in the time of my grandfather? I do not only say, what man's was it? but what nation's? The astrologer tells me of Saturn and Mars in opposition; but I say, let them be as they will, their courses and their positions are ordered them by an unchangeable decree of fate.

Either they produce and point out the effects of all things, or else they signify them; if the former, what are we the better for the knowledge of that which must of necessity come to pass? If the latter, what does it avail us to foresee what we cannot avoid? So that whether we know or not know, the event will still be the same.

He that designs the institution of human life should not be over-curious of his words; it does not stand with his dignity to be solicitous about sounds and syllables, and to debase the mind of man with trivial things; placing wisdom in matters that are rather difficult than great. If it be eloquent, it is his good fortune, not his business. Subtle disputations are only the sport of wits that play upon the catch, and are fitter to be contemned than resolved.

Were not I a madman to sit wrangling about words, and putting of nice and impertinent questions, when the enemy has already made the breach, the town fired over my head, and the mine ready to play that shall blow me up into the air? Were this a time for fooleries? Let me rather fortify myself against death and inevitable necessities; let me understand that the good of life does not consist in the length or space, but in the use of it. When I go to sleep, who knows whether I shall ever wake again? And when I wake, whether ever I shall sleep again? When I go abroad, whether ever I shall come home again? And when I return, whether ever I shall go abroad again? It is not at sea only that life and death are within a few inches one of another; but they are as near everywhere else too, only we do not take so much notice of it.

What have we to do with frivolous and captious questions, and impertinent niceties? Let us rather study how to deliver ourselves from sadness, fear, and the burden of all our secret lusts: let us pass over all our most solemn levities, and make haste to a good life, which is a thing that presses us. Shall a man that goes for a midwife, stand gaping upon a post to see what play to-day? Or, when his house is on fire, stay the curling of a periwig before he calls for help? Our houses are on fire, our country invaded, our goods taken away, our children in danger; and, I might add to these, the calamities of earthquakes, shipwrecks, and whatever else is most terrible. Is this a time for us now to be playing fast and loose with idle questions, which are in effect so many unprofitable riddles? Our duty is the cure of the mind rather than the delight of it; but we have only the words of wisdom without the works; and turn philosophy into a pleasure that was given for a remedy. What can be more ridiculous than for a man to neglect his manners and compose his style? We are sick and ulcerous, and must be lanced and scarified, and every man has as much business within himself as a physician in a common pestilence.

"Misfortunes," in fine, "cannot be avoided; but they may be sweetened, if not overcome; and our lives may be made happy by philosophy."

ON A HAPPY LIFE

Seneca

		Qty
ISBN: 9781920785949		
RRP	AU$15.99	.....
Postage within Australia	AU$5.00	.....
	TOTAL★ $_____	
	★ All prices include GST	

Name: ....

Address: ....

....

Phone: ....

Email: ....

Payment: [ ] Money Order   [ ] Cheque   [ ] MasterCard   [ ] Visa

Cardholder's Name:...

Credit Card Number: ....

Signature:..

Expiry Date: ....

Allow 7 days for delivery.

Payment to: Marzocco Consultancy (ABN 14 067 257 390)
PO Box 452
Torquay Victoria 3228
Australia

BE PUBLISHED

Publish through a successful publisher.
Brolga Publishing is represented through:
• National book trade distribution, including sales,
marketing & distribution through Simon & Schuster.
• International book trade distribution to:
- The United Kingdom
- Sales representation in South East Asia
• Worldwide e-Book distribution

For details and enquiries, contact:
Brolga Publishing Pty Ltd
ABN 46 063 962 443
PO Box 452
Torquay Victoria 3228
Australia

markzocchi@brolgapublishing.com.au
(Email for a catalogue request)